BOOK 1

REVISED EDITION

Tunes You Like

Your Favorite Songs Made Easy to Play

Arranged For Piano Solo By
Mark Nevin

CONTENTS

Associated Music Publishers, Inc.

DISTRIBUTED BY
HAL•LEONARD
CORPORATION
7777 W. BLUEMOUND RD. P.O. BOX 13819 MILWAUKEE, WI 53213

ISBN 0-7935-0686-7

Yankee Doodle

Moderato

Arranged by Mark Nevin

Yan - kee Doo - dle went to town rid - ing on a pon - y Stuck a feath - er in his hat and called it mac - a - ro - ni.

Mary Had a Little Lamb

Moderato

Arranged by Mark Nevin

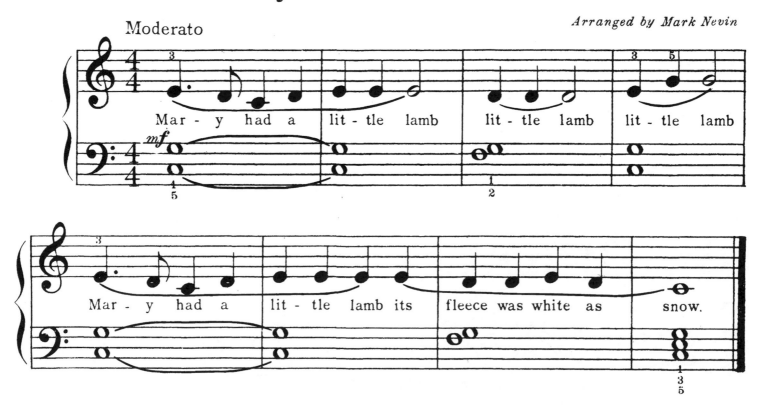

Mar - y had a lit - tle lamb lit - tle lamb lit - tle lamb Mar - y had a lit - tle lamb its fleece was white as snow.

Old Mac Donald Had a Farm

Arranged by Mark Nevin

London Bridge

Arranged by Mark Nevin

Lazy Mary

Arranged by Mark Nevin

Comin' Round the Mountain

SOUTHERN MOUNTAIN SONG
Arranged by Mark Nevin

She'll be com-in' round the moun-tain when she comes

She'll be com-in' round the moun-tain when she comes

She'll be com-in' round the moun-tain, She'll be com-in' round the

moun-tain, She'll be com-in' round the moun-tain when she comes.

Frere Jacques
(ARE YOU SLEEPING?)

FRENCH MELODY
Arranged by Mark Nevin

Alouette

FRENCH SONG
Arranged by Mark Nevin

A - lou-et - te, gen-tille A-lou-et - te, A - lou-et - te je te plu-me - rai.

America
(MY COUNTRY 'TIS OF THEE)

SAMUEL FRANCIS SMITH

HENRY CAREY
Arranged by Mark Nevin

Moderato

My coun-try 'tis of thee, Sweet land of lib - er - ty,

Of thee I sing. Land where my fa - thers died, Land of the

Pil - grims' pride, From ev - 'ry moun-tain side, Let free - dom ring.

Twinkle, Twinkle Little Star

Arranged by Mark Nevin

The Farmer in the Dell

Moderato

Arranged by Mark Nevin

The farm-er in the dell, ___ the farm-er in the dell, ___
The farm-er takes a wife, ___ the farm-er takes a wife, ___

Heigh ho the der-ry O the farm-er in the dell. ___
Heigh ho the der-ry O the farm-er takes a wife. ___

The wife takes a child, ___ the wife takes a child, ___

Heigh ho the der-ry O the wife takes a child. ___

Cradle Song
(BRAHMS LULLABY)

JOHANNES BRAHMS
Arranged by Mark Nevin

Jingle Bells

Arranged by Mark Nevin

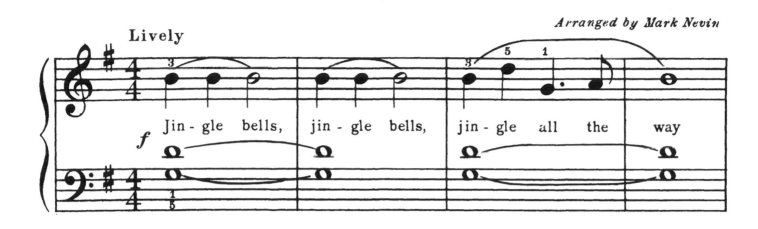

Jin - gle bells, jin - gle bells, jin - gle all the way

Oh, what fun it is to ride in a one horse op - en sleigh

Jin - gle bells, jin - gle bells, jin - gle all the way

Oh, what fun it is to ride in a one horse op - en sleigh.

Silent Night

FRANZ GRUBER
Arranged by Mark Nevin

Andante

Si - lent night, ho - ly night, All is calm, all is bright, Round yon vir - gin moth - er and child, Ho - ly in - fant so ten - der and mild, Sleep in hea - ven - ly peace, Sleep in hea - ven - ly peace.

Adeste Fideles
(O COME, ALL YE FAITHFUL)

JOHN READING

Arranged by Mark Nevin

O come, all ye faith-ful, joy-ful and tri - um -phant, O

come ye, O come ye to Beth - le - hem.

Come and be - hold Him, born the King of an - gels, O

come, let us a - dore Him, O come, let us a - dore Him, O

come, let us a - dore Him, Christ the Lord.

Home on the Range

AMERICAN COWBOY SONG
Arranged by Mark Nevin

Moderato

Home, home on the range, _____ Where the

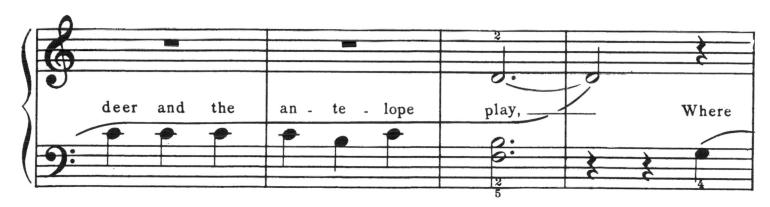

deer and the an - te - lope play, _____ Where

sel - dom is heard a dis - cour - ag - ing word, And the

skies are not cloud - y all day. _____

Old Folks at Home
(SWANEE RIVER)

STEPHEN FOSTER
Arranged by Mark Nevin

The Mulberry Bush

Moderato

Arranged by Mark Nevin

Oh, dark-ies how my heart grows wear-y far from de old folks at home.

Here we go 'round the mul-ber-ry bush, the mul-ber-ry bush, the mul-ber-ry bush,

Here we go 'round the mul-ber-ry bush, So ear-ly in the morn-ing.

This is the way we wash our clothes, we wash our clothes, we wash our clothes,

This is the way we wash our clothes, So ear-ly Mon-day morn-ing.

The Star Spangled Banner

FRANCIS SCOTT KEY
Moderato

JOHN STAFFORD SMITH
Arranged by Mark Nevin

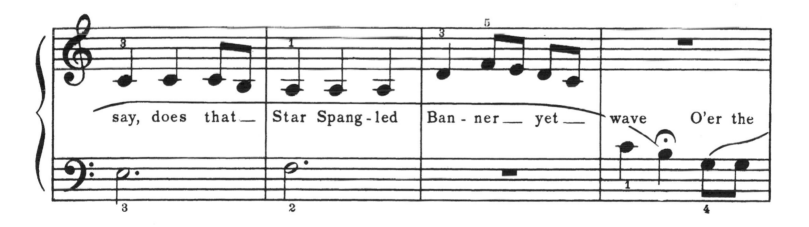

Auld Lang Syne

SCOTCH MELODY
Arranged by Mark Nevin

Three Blind Mice

Arranged by Mark Nevin

Dixie

DAN EMMETT
Arranged by Mark Nevin

Land. Den I wish I was in Dix - ie, Hoo - ray! Hoo -

ray! In Dix - ie Land I'll take my stand to lib and die in

Dix - ie, A - way, a - way, a - way down south in

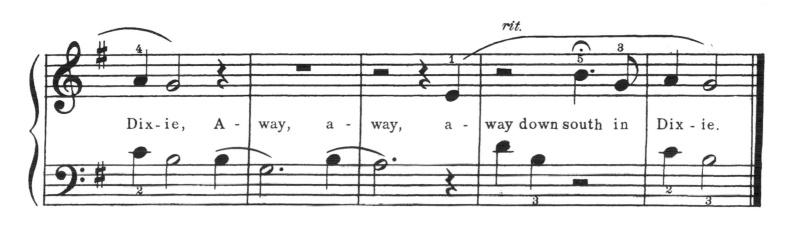

Dix - ie, A - way, a - way, a - way down south in Dix - ie.

rit.